Pebble® Plus

Celebrating Differences

We All Come from
Different Cultures

by Melissa Higgins

raintree

a Capstone company — publishers for children

Raintree is an imprint of Capstone Global Library Limited, a company incorporated in England and Wales having its registered office at 264 Banbury Road, Oxford, OX2 7DY – Registered company number: 6695582

www.raintree.co.uk
myorders@raintree.co.uk

Jeni Wittrock, editor; Gene Bentdahl, designer; Svetlana Zhurkin, media researcher; Kathy McColley, production specialist; Marcy Morin, photo scheduler; Sarah Schuette, photo stylist

ISBN 978 1 4747 2362 6
20 19 18 17 16
10 9 8 7 6 5 4 3 2 1

British Library Cataloguing in Publication Data
A full catalogue record for this book is available from the British Library.

Acknowledgements
We would like to thank the following for permission to reproduce photographs: Alamy: LHB Photo, 1; Dreamstime: Distinctiveimages, 17, Jose Gil, 9, Noam Armonn, 15; iStockphoto: Christopher Futcher, 5; Shutterstock: Blend Images, 13, iofoto, 21, Shestakoff, 19, Stanislaw Tokarski, 7, Zurijeta, Cover; Svetlana Zhurkin, 11

We would like to thank Gail Saunders Smith, PhD and Donna Barkman, Children's Literature Specialist and Diversity Consultantant Ossining, New York for their invaluable help in the preparation of this book.

Every effort has been made to contact copyright holders of material reproduced in this book. Any omissions will be rectified in subsequent printings if notice is given to the publisher.

All the internet addresses (URLs) given in this book were valid at the time of going to press. However, due to the dynamic nature of the internet, some addresses may have changed, or sites may have changed or ceased to exist since publication. While the author and publisher regret any inconvenience this may cause readers, no responsibility for any such changes can be accepted by either the author or the publisher.

Note to parents and teachers

This book describes and illustrates differences in cultures. The images support early readers in understanding the text. The repetition of words and phrases helps early readers to learn new words. This book also introduces early readers to subject-specific vocabulary words, which are defined in the Glossary. Early readers may need assistance to read some words and to use the Contents, Glossary, Read more and Index sections of the book.

Made in China

Contents

Different cultures

People come from many
different cultures.
We are all friends.

Celebrating traditions

My parents come from Poland.
Sometimes I do traditional
Polish dancing with my friends.
Our costumes are bright and
colourful!

Chinese New Year lasts for two weeks. A dancing dragon and popping firecrackers bring good luck to everyone.

A pavada is a dress

young girls wear in India.

I feel proud to wear these

traditional clothes.

11

My ancestors came from Africa many years ago. Now I am learning African drumming at school.

Sharing customs

I love to eat Middle Eastern food with my friends. Falafel sandwiches are the best.

My family is from Southeast

Asia. I am learning Arabic

so that I can read the Koran.

17

My name is Philippa. My name means "someone who likes horses". I love horses!

We like being different

Being different is fun.

It's great to share our

different customs.

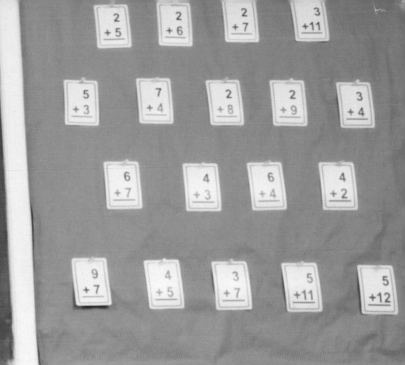

21

Glossary

ancestor family member who lived a long time ago

culture beliefs, customs and way of life

costumes clothes worn by people at a particular time or in a particular place

tradition a custom, idea or belief passed down through time

Read more

Families Around the World (Around the World), Clare Lewis (Raintree, 2014)

Millennium Children of Britain Just Like Me, Barnabas and Anabel Kindersley (Dorling Kindersley, 1999)

People of the World (Go Go Global), Nancy Loewen and Paula Skelley (Raintree, 2015)

Sammi and Dusty (City Farm), Jessie Williams (Curious Fox, 2013)

We Are All Different, Rebecca Rissman (Raintree, 2011)

What I Like About Me! A Book Celebrating Differences, Allia Zobel-Nolan (Reader's Digest Children's Books, 2005)

Index